THE PERFECT SALES CALL

Tony Morris

CGW
PUBLISHING

2015

The Perfect Sales Call

First Edition: April 2015

ISBN 978-01-908293-33-6

© Tony Morris 2015

Published by:

CGW Publishing
B 1502
PO Box 15113
Birmingham
B2 2NJ
United Kingdom

www.cgwpublishing.com

mail@cgwpublishing.com

Being in sales can be a very frustrating job; it takes an enormous amount of will power, self discipline and self motivation to keep pushing yourself when times are tough.

Some salespeople have to juggle these emotions alongside difficulties in their personal life; which can make things seem impossible.

I on the other hand, have the exact opposite. I have been blessed with the most loving, supportive, caring and selfless wife any man could ever ask for. Like many business owners, I work most evenings and at least a quarter of my weekend and I never hear a moan, in fact she often praises my hard work and determination.

When I hit a tough patch and start to doubt myself, she is always in my corner motivating me and spurring me on and giving me the reassurance I crave.

She is not just my wife and mother of my children, she is my best friend, my soul mate and my everything.

Thank you Shana for being you every day; please never change.

Contents

1: MIND SET

"If you're going to have an attitude, you may as well have a positive one." I heard that about 16 years ago when I first started selling utilities in a call centre and it's stuck with me ever since; I have taken huge value from it.

Think for one second, what benefits do you gain from thinking negative thoughts and having a negative mind set? I am yet to think of one benefit that can be gained from that exercise; however there are plenty from having a positive mind set.

You know when you're in the midst of a heated row with your loved one or a friend and you really struggle to get your point across as you are so angry and you just see red. However, an hour later when the situation has calmed down, you're miraculously able to come up with things you should and could have said to win the argument. There is a very simple reason for this; when you are angry and in a negative state, you block any positive messages and ideas in your mind. It's only when you are taken out of that situation or environment, that your mind is able to wander and come up with sensible suggestions and ideas.

In the 9 years that I have run Sales Doctors, my sales training company, I have been fortunate to train over 3,000 sales professionals. When I analyse the top 1% in terms of consistent best performers, the one thing they all have in common is a positive mind set. That doesn't mean if they have a bad week, they'll just write it off and say next week will be better. They will focus on what they DID ACHIEVE in that bad week, as opposed to what most negative people do and focus on all the things they DID NOT ACHIEVE. If their goal was to do prospecting over the phone and make 10 new business appointments and they only generated 2, they will focus on how many new prospects they came across of value. They will look at how many decision makers' names they managed to identify during their call outs. They will look at the companies they were able to qualify out as they didn't fit the criteria of the sort of business they want to work with, so they don't have to invest their time and energy in them again. The key point is they will always look at the positive in everything they do, as they understand there is no value or benefit gained in looking at the negative.

There's an old story of a shoe manufacturer that sent two of their sales team out to Africa to sell their new range of shoes. A couple of days later, one of the sales consultants called the boss and the conversation went like this:

Boss: Hi Jeff, how are you getting on?

Jeff: Are you insane? Why on Earth did you send me out here?

Boss: What are you talking about it, what's the issue?

Jeff: I've got no chance, I may as well come home now; I've got absolutely no chance, literally no one wears any shoes!!!

A few hours later, the other sales guy calls the boss and the conversation goes something like this:

Boss: Hi Pete, how's things going for you?

Pete: I want to thank you with all my heart; you must have so much faith in me and you're the best boss I've ever had the fortune to work for

Boss: Well I'm delighted to hear that, why are you thanking me?

Pete: I have the best opportunity in the World, you're going to need to send me more stock, it's unreal, literally no one wears any shoes!!!

How would you have viewed the situation? Would you have thought like Jeff or Pete?

Some people are naturally positive people and being up beat comes quite easily for them, for others it's a real struggle. However, there are proven ways to get you in a positive mind set.

Here are just some of the things that have worked for my clients:

1. Listen to an uplifting song on the way to work and before a sales meeting

2. Do some exercise first thing in the morning to release the endorphins – if time is an issue, get up earlier; it's really easy to make excuses, much harder doing things that will actually benefit you

3. Spend a few minutes doing something you enjoy each morning i.e. playing with your kids, take the dog for a walk, have a coffee and a cigarette, watch a few minutes of your favourite comedy program, have a relaxing walk

4. Give yourself enough time to get ready and have breakfast

5. Write a list of all the things you're grateful for

6. Look at the goals you have set yourself for the next 3 to 6 months

7. Stare at the mood board you have created of all the material items you are striving for

8. Look back at your successful sales months to remind yourself that you can achieve and you are successful at what you do

Different things will work for different people, as we are all motivated by a variation of different things. The key is to take action and do something that puts you in a positive place, so when you go into work, you do so with the mindset that today is going to be a successful one.

In the box below, write down what you are going to implement to ensure you are in a positive frame of mind:

One thing I adore about sales is there is no such thing as failure, it's all feedback. What lesson can you take away from each situation that will make you better, more rounded sales professional?

I am sure you have read thousands of positive quotes in the past; however my favourite is from an inspirational American football coach by the name Vince Lombardi. He managed a team called the Green Bay Packers and one of my favourite quotes of his is "My team have never lost a game; they just ran out of time".

2: IT'S NOT WHAT YOU SAY, IT'S HOW YOU SAY IT

If you had to explain to someone in one word, what sales is, what would you say? My word would be COMMUNICATION. Ultimately sales is communicating a message with an end goal in mind; whether that's to make an appointment, educate someone, persuade someone to follow your advice etc.

There was a study carried out in the 1960s by two researchers named Mehrabian and Argyle into the meaning of communication. This pie chart represents their findings.

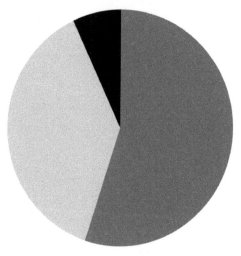

In the pie chart, the three areas represent the following:

1. The words we use
2. How we say the words
3. Body language

Any idea which percentage is applied to which area?

The words we use: 7%

How we say the words: 38%

Body language: 55%

What I find interesting about these findings is that the majority of communication is non verbal. Over the phone, you don't have the benefit of body language, so think how vital it is that you sound right.

About a year ago I was cold called by a lady trying to sell me sales leads for my company. She had a good opening gambit and she had clearly researched my business, however I interrupted her pitch and asked her, "are you depressed?" In a shocked voice, she replied, "what do you mean?" I repeated, "are you depressed?" She apologised and in a confused tone said, "I don't understand why you're asking me that?" Now granted I was a being difficult for the sake of it, however I wanted to make a point with her and I informed her that she sounded depressed. I told her she had absolutely no chance of achieving the goal she had set out for herself, because she sounded like her world had ended. She started to level with me and explained that she had been calling a list of training companies and I was on that list and she was having a pretty unsuccessful day. She admitted, without saying it, that she was expecting a no before picking up the phone; I mean what chance did she have? We ended up having a good chat and her company is now a client of mine. You don't think I'd miss a sales opportunity like that did you?

In almost every call centre in the country you'll see great big signs up saying, "Smile when you dial" and, "don't moan when you pick up the phone". Although these are extremely cheesy and very old school, they still serve a purpose. Be honest with yourself, do you sound up for it on every single phone call?

When I train my clients to make a sales call, I tell them to visualise a big bubble around them and block out all the noise around them and get into a zone. They do their brief research, which I'll expand on later and they get themselves in a comfortable posture, they ensure they have all the resources they possibly need and they make their call. If you don't sound enthused, how can you possibly expect to enthuse the person you're speaking with.

Every sales call could be the best opportunity of your career. How do you know when you're going to get hold of the whale and generate an opportunity which could be the highest value deal you ever create.

I want you to take a minute now and think of the biggest deal you've done to date in your sales career, that you personally self generated.

Now think back when you made your first contact with one or the main decision maker?

How did you sound on that phone call? Did you sound depressed? I very much doubt you did!

3: GATEKEEPERS

The amusing thing is these gatekeepers or Rottweilers, as you might call them, have been trained to stop sales people getting through.

Most sales people are under the impression they have to speak to them in a certain way, normally with no respect and that will be enough to get past them. This could not be further from the truth. So the first thing is to treat them like a human being, and ask for their help and they'll normally, not always, respond positively. Be as friendly, charming and sincere as you can and you might shock yourself!

One very common objection a gatekeeper may give you is, 'no name policy', therefore if you haven't got the contact's name, they can't put you through. With the genius invention of LinkedIn that has eliminated 90% of these cases. Type into LinkedIn the name of the company and then there is a tab for employees; it will provide a few names and if your chosen contact isn't there then call up and say "I have spoken to X and he wasn't the right person, who would you recommend?"

If you can't find the full name on LinkedIn, use Google by typing in: Sales Director (your target company) LinkedIn and this will take you straight to the Sales Directors page. An alternative I use to LinkedIn is Duedil; this is free of charge and contains Companies House information.

Failing that, here are some more ways to overcome the no name policy:

1. Make up a name – "Good Morning can I speak to Mike Beard please?"

   We don't have a Mike Beard here. I have him down as the Sales Director, who has taken over his position? (John Smith they say).

2. "Hi, it's Tony here from (a business directory) and I am just updating my records. Is Mike Beard still the Sales Director?", "He's not, who's taken over his role? Great can I just get his email address and mobile please for my data."

3. Visit their website – there will usually be a name mentioned somewhere in meet the team, the news pages or see who writes their blog. It might not be the contact you are after, however you can use that name when you call back.

4. Be aware of the times to call. If you do have the Directors names but the gatekeeper won't put you through call during times the gatekeeper is unlikely to be there:

Before 08:45

12:15 – 13:45

After 17:30

5. Make a joke of the no name response. This must be done with charm and wit or you will get called a variety of rude names like I have in the past. So when the gatekeeper says "I'm afraid it's a no name policy" simply respond "I understand that, and sorry, who am I speaking with?" "Michelle" she replies. I think you may have just broken your policy Michelle!! I normally get "good one d**k head" and the lovely sound of a dead phone line; however it's worked on occasion.

6. Gatekeepers are trained to ask "are they expecting your call?" Your response must always be "I'm returning their call."

7. If you have the contact name and the gatekeeper asks, "Is this a cold call or a new business call?" "No, I am returning their call." Always ask for your contact by their first name, as this gives the impression you know them personally.

8. Ask for their help. Most people actually like to help when they are spoken to in the right way.

Write down which techniques from the above appeal to you personally and start using them:

4: OPENING STATEMENT

When making the perfect sales call, what's one thing you can guarantee from the receiver's perspective? He or she is going to be busy. They will be busy in a meeting, preparing for a meeting or busy at work; therefore we are disturbing them no matter what. So when preparing that call, it's imperative that all you are thinking about is WIIFM – What's In It For Me?, the 'me' being the receiver of the call, your prospective customer. What I mean by 'what's in it for me?' is what am I getting out of this call.

An opening statement is often referred to as an 'elevator pitch'. Imagine you are in an elevator and your ideal prospective customer walks into the elevator and asks 'what do you do?' You now have 10 to 15 seconds to say something that will engage, inspire and entice that person to say 'that sounds interesting, tell me more'. Unless you are in the elevator in the Shard in London where you will have around 3 hours!

So when preparing your opening statement, gambit, elevator pitch, whatever you wish to call it, there are a few things you need to think about to achieve your desired effect. I got cold called very recently by a gentleman trying to sell me marketing programmes for my sales training company; his tone of voice was good and he sounded enthusiastic, however the message was irrelevant to me. He told me his company had been established for 27 years (irrelevant to me), he told me they specialise in digital marketing programmes (irrelevant to me) and that he had worked with other sales training companies (this was the only thing that caught my attention). Although what he failed to tell me, which would have been the most important piece of information to me, is HOW he helped the other sales training companies. The end result is all that I and other business owners want to hear, but without this information, it's all irrelevant.

There are a few stages to preparing your opening statement:

1: Objective

What is your objective of the call? You need to think about what do you want to happen as a result of the phone call. If, you're looking to make appointments with the decision maker, then you need to prepare at least two dates that you're available to meet that person.

2: Know their market

You need to understand what the company you are calling actually does. Now I am not suggesting you do 15 minutes research, because you could end up leaving a voice mail, which would not be the most productive use of your time; however you need to look at their website for at least a minute to grasp what they do. You can then look at your clients that you have worked with that are similar to them; either competitors of theirs or would have similar requirement to them.

3: Talk results

This is by far the most important stage of the opening statement. When making that perfect sales call, do NOT talk about what you do, talk about what you have done, successfully, with companies or people like them. Remember, people only care about how you can help them or their business, so the result is everything. So look at the clients you have worked with who are similar to them and then make a note of the results you have achieved for them.

4: Your first question

Once you have delivered your opening statement, you need to get the prospect talking; the only way to do that is ask a well planned open question that will engage him or her. You need to therefore think about the information you would like to obtain, whilst ensuring it's going to create a need for your product or service.

5: Write and rehearse

This is the second most important stage of the opening statement. You need to write it out and you need to practice it and say it out aloud at least 5 times so its flows and sounds natural, not scripted.

Let me show you an example of an opening statement I would use for when calling an estate agent. Obviously, I haven't included stage 5 because the whole thing is written down for you to rehearse!

1: Objective

When calling an estate agent my goal is to make a qualified appointment with the decision maker.

2: Know their market

I know this estate agent I am calling does both sales and lettings. I'm aware of the number of branches they have, an approximate size of their team and the area they cover. I have already found three competitors who I have trained that are a similar size to them. An important point here is to not name drop companies too large that will make you look too big or vice versa.

3: Talk results

As I have worked with their competition, I'm aware of key challenges they faced e.g. lack of stock to rent and constantly being pushed on their fees; therefore it's likely these challenges will be relevant to the agency I will be calling.

4: Your first question

As I know lack of stock to rent is a major issue with many estate agents I train, I will create a question that will highlight this problem, as I have a solution up my sleeve.

Now this is what I would say:

"Good morning John (always use their first name and avoid Sir or madam), thanks for taking my call (do not ask is it convenient to speak, it allows them to say no). My name is Tony Morris and I am the Director of Sales Doctor. Are you familiar with my business?"

"Yes" – Great, as you are probably aware...

OR

"No" – OK, to make you aware...

"We have been successfully helping many estate agents such as (name drop ones they'd have heard of) by teaching sales negotiators to build more value, therefore achieving a higher fee and providing them with ideas to gain private landlords details and calling them, resulting in a significant increase in instructions to let.

In this market our clients have found one of the biggest challenges they face is lack of stock, how have you found this at the moment?" (Very likely to be the same if it's a big problem for the majority).

"At this stage I don't know if we can help you as well, so can you help me by telling me...." (This is a good take away phrase, as you are not guaranteeing you can help them, however it's allowing you to ask some questions to see if you can)

"How are you pro-actively increasing your rental stock?" (Good open question to get them talking about a problem their competitors have)

Let me show you another example I have created for a client of mine that sells promotional merchandise:

"Good morning John, thanks for taking my call. My name is Tony Morris from (company). Have you heard of us before?"

"Yes" – Great, as you already might know...

"No" – OK, to make you aware...

"We specialise in offering creative solutions for your promotional needs..."

✓ John, this enables you to increase your brand awareness whilst freeing up you time to do other things

✓ John, this enables you to increase your revenue whilst taking away any headache

✓ John, this enables you to increase your revenue whilst saving money at the same time

Then... SHUT UP & LET THEM TALK

"At this stage John, I don't know if I can do the same for you. So can you help me by telling me...

"What promotional merchandise have you used in the past?"

"What were your objectives when using this merchandise?"

"What results did you achieve from it?""

An easy way to remember how to plan a call is GAP; this stands for:

Goal	Goal or objective of the call
Angle	The angle you're going to take
Prepare	Preparation of what you're going to say, your environment etc.

Now I want you to plan a call to someone on your hit list (this is a list of companies that you should have created that you want to work with; if you haven't created it, it's not too late to start now). Break down the call into 4 stages:

1: Objective

Write in the box your clear objective of the call:

2: Know their market

Write in the box what you know about this company:

[empty box]

Which companies have you worked with that are similar to them:

[empty box]

3: Talk results

What results have you achieved with similar companies to them? Think about your product/ service offering and ask yourself the following questions:

1. What would a prospect gain from using my products or services? e.g. more efficiency, increase conversions, a more streamlined process.

2. What will they reduce or avoid by using your products/ services? e.g. reduce their cost per lead, reduce the time to manage their system, avoid repair and maintenance costs. Once you know the key benefits that are the most important to your prospect, you are able to add this part to your opening statement.

4: Your first question

Open questions that will engage them and get them talking about a problem that you can fix:

Once you have answered these 4 stages, you are now ready to write your opening statement:

Voicemails

Now there have been many debates in sales whether to leave voice mails, and if so, what do you say?

I get approx 60 % of people call me back from a cold call and my voice mail is very straight forward and I have named it 'the ambiguous voice mail'.

"Hi Steve, its Tony. Give us a bell back on 07915 *** ***. Thanks".

Do not state your surname, your company name or the reason for your call. By using the informal language the prospect falls into the trap and returns your call from curiosity alone. You may be thinking I wouldn't return that voice mail and you may be right and then you would fall into that 40%. If you don't try, you'll never know.

5: Building Rapport

Kerry Johnson, the professional tennis player and author of Selling with NLP (Neuro Linguistic Programming) defines building rapport as "the bridge that helps the person you are communicating with find meaning and intent in the things you say".

So what is building rapport all about? It's about making people comfortable, finding common ground with people and creating a short term relationship.

People like to deal with people like them, so we need to act more like them, through the sales process. This technique is known as 'matching'.

So over the phone how do we match people? These are the key things to listen out for and match:

- Pace – the speed at which someone talks

- Pitch – how high or how low a voice is

- Timbre – the resonance of a voice

- Word inflections and accents – different ways to pronounce the same word

- Language - use the same words as the prospect i.e. if they say they are, "looking for hassle free process", then do not translate that to, "with us it's convenient".

Record personal information about your client and bring it up in ongoing correspondence e.g. hobbies, mutual contacts, children's names.

Think of your top 10 clients right now. In the box below, fill in details that you know about them personally that you can use in your next correspondence:

Name	Personal Information
1	
2	
3	
4	

Name	Personal Information
5	
6	
7	
8	
9	
10	

If you struggled with that exercise, then you need to go away and start showing more of an interest in your clients and finding out more about them on a personal level. Some clients will be introverted behaviour and not wish to share things with you and you must respect this, however you can still show an interest in their business when they have their annual anniversary or win awards that you can read about on their website or social media page.

As I demonstrated in that earlier diagram of the study of communication by Mehrabian and Argyle; the majority of communication is non verbal.

Over the phone you don't have the luxury of using body language, therefore how we sound becomes even more important. I received a cold call recently from a guy selling a free website review for my business; his opening statement went like this:

"Hi is that Tony?"

"Yes", I replied, "who is this?"

"My name is Joe Bloggs calling from X websites and the reason for my call is to offer you a free website review for your website. Would that be of interest to you?"

I hope by now you can spot the many flaws in his pitch; to name but a few:

1. No what's in it for me

2. No benefit statement of how this website review will help my business

3. Awful closed question at the end

4. No personalisation; I was clearly just another lead on his list

5. Not a single open question to show any interest in me or my business

6. No demonstration that he even understood what I did

My response to his question, would that be of interest to you? was probably unnecessary, however I wanted to teach him a valuable lesson. I replied to him by asking, "are you depressed?" In a confused voice he said, "excuse me?" I repeated "Are you depressed? Because you sound it". He admitted that he was having a bad day and that he hadn't organised a single website review and was starting to panic. I appreciated his honesty, however if you think about it, he was making his life harder by already expecting a "No" before picking up the phone. He was relying on pure luck, as opposed to skilled salesman ship to gain a commitment.

When you rely on luck, you might as well try your hand at gambling, not selling.

6: QUESTIONING

One of the most important parts of sales is questioning. The better your questioning, the better understanding of your prospects needs, and therefore giving you the best chance of recommending the right products/ services to them.

Why do we ask open questions?

- To gain information
- To show an interest in your prospect/ customer
- To make them comfortable
- To be thorough
- To build rapport
- To get your prospect/ customer to talk (80/20)
- To demonstrate your credibility
- To gain their trust
- To understand their needs

Let me illustrate this. You walk into a Doctor's surgery and see Doctor number one and say, "Doctor I hope you can help, I have a splitting headache." He replies, "take some Paracetamol and if the pain persists please come back and see me."

I then walk in and see Doctor two and say, "I hope you can help," I have a splitting headache. The doctor offers me a seat and says:

Dr: Where in your head is the pain?

Me: In my temples.

Dr: When in the day do you get these headaches?

Me: Normally the morning.

Dr: How long have you been suffering?

Me: About a month in total.

Dr: How much liquid do you drink in a day?

Me: About a litre I guess.

Dr: On a scale of one to 10, 10 being excruciating pain, where would you describe your pain?

Me: I suppose a 7 at its worst.

Dr: From what you've described I would recommend Paracetamol, if the pain persists come back and see me.

Which Doctor would you rather see?

I would assume the latter would be your answer.

Which Doctor is better medically trained? Really we don't know, they could be as qualified as each other.

So why did you choose Doctor 2? What did he demonstrate that the first Doctor didn't?

He showed his credibility, clearly took an interest in me, gave me absolute confidence that he knew what he was doing. So by asking a few open questions, my perception was, he was far more professional and a much better Doctor.

A good way to remember the six open questions:

"I keep six honest serving men, they taught me all I knew; their names are What and Why and When and How and Where and Who."

Rudyard Kipling, from Just So Stories, 1902

Before a call, I recommend that you have a list of good open questions in front of you to ask the prospect so you are best prepared, in case they put you on the spot. You should always keep the seven open questions in front of you.

What

Why

When

How

Where

Who

Which

These questions can be thought provoking, problem questions, situation questions, power questions etc. let me show you some examples.

Power questions

Here are some examples if you sell:

Pagers - If your most important client desperately needed to get hold of you and you were in a meeting, how would you get the message?

Satellite television – If you owned your own cable company, what channels would you put on it?

Sales training – How many of your sales people did not reach their targets last year?

What was the major cause of that?

What plans have you got in place to ensure they meet them this year?

How do you support your sales staff?

What are your sales teams biggest challenges?

What have you got in place to help overcome these?

Out of your 10 sales people, who is normally your top performer? (John) and who is often at the bottom? (Mike); In your valued opinion, what does John have that Mike hasn't?

Decision maker questions

How will the decision be made?

Aside from yourself John, who else gets involved in making the decision?

In the past, how were these decisions made and who was involved in them?

What are your key priorities in order to make this decision?

Thought provoking questions

What would you do Mr. Prospect if you lost your two biggest clients?

Now let me ask you, what have you got in place to keep them?

Situation questions

How long have you been responsible for managing the sales team?

What has been your favourite role prior to this position?

Where do you see yourself in the next 5 years?

Problem questions

What 3 key areas do you feel your current supplier could improve?

What are you not getting, that you would like?

On a scale of 1 – 10, 10 being exceptional service, how would you rate your current supplier? (answer 7) What's required to make them a 10?

If there was one thing that would make you consider looking elsewhere, what would it be?

Leading questions

What do you like about this property?

What do you dislike?

What jumped out at you from this brochure?

In the tables below I want you to write a list of 4 open questions that you will now start using on the phone for each of the different questions.

Power questions

1
2
3
4

Decision maker questions

1
2
3
4

Thought provoking questions

1	
2	
3	
4	

Situation questions

1	
2	
3	
4	

Problem questions

1
2
3
4

Leading questions

1
2
3
4

7: LISTENING

In sales we are often reminded that we have two ears and one mouth, however, sales people often act like it's the other way around. People are interested in what **they** have to say, so let them talk. On the perfect sales call, you should be aiming to speak around 20% to 30% of the call. Be really honest and ask yourself, on average, what percentage are you speaking?

Sales people try and argue this point and say they have lots of information to share, therefore they are required to speak more; however, how much of the information is actually relevant to the prospect? Equally, is it important that we share the information on the phone or in a face to face meeting? I appreciate this depends on your objective of the call, and whether you're looking to make a sale or set up an appointment, however be careful to not bombard your prospect and share information that does NOT need to be shared.

Listening is a skill and it does not come easily to most, especially sales people, so here are a few ways designed to improve the important art of listening.

Use tag on questions

So when the prospect says, "that price is one factor of the decision making process" you could reply by asking, "what are the other factors involved in making the decision?"

Repeat things back to the prospect

Once you let the prospect speak, say, "I think what you are saying is a,b,c and d; is that right"

Summarise at the end

Towards the end of the telephone call say, "to ensure I haven't missed anything, you are looking to partner a company that can achieve a, b, c and d, is that right?"

Active listening

People hate talking to themselves; so make the prospect aware you're listening by making acknowledgement sounds like ummm, urrr, that's interesting, I see etc.

Asking questions

Ask the prospect questions related to what they have discussed.

Examples

Use examples to illustrate you have expertise in what the prospect is discussing i.e. I had another estate agent client that had the same challenge, we were able to solve that in a matter of 3 weeks by implementing 4 key strategies that I will talk to you about in a meeting.

Language

In any future correspondence, use exactly the same language that your prospect uses to demonstrate you have listened.

Acknowledgement

I am really pleased you asked me Mr Prospect about our biggest USPs.

Key dates

Make a diary note of any important things the prospect discusses on the call and then you can call or email the client to congratulate them or to discuss how things went.

In the table below, write down 10 things you're pro-actively going to do to improve your listening skills when making the perfect sales call:

1	
2	
3	
4	
5	
6	
7	
8	
9	
10	

One of the most important things to listen out for are buying signals. These are any indicators that the prospect is interested in what you have to say. They are often questions that the prospect might ask such as, "how long is the contract for?" To determine if its a buying signal, you should ask yourself, why are they asking me this question? Many sales people miss these, so make sure you're not one of them!

8: HANDLE THE PERSON, NOT THE OBJECTION

Inevitably when making your perfect sales call, objections will arise. Many sales people are taught, how to overcome the objection; the problem with this is, if you overcome an objection and win, then your prospect loses and no one likes to be a loser.

I believe in sales today, its about handling the person, not the objection and getting the person to see things your way. Once you can help people's see things your way, then you are able to help them buy from you, as opposed to sell to them. Let me give you a great example of this: if someone says 'let me think about it' this generic response could mean a number of things; it could mean they need more time before making a decision, it could mean they need to discuss it with their business partner, they might need to go and compare it to your competitors . The point is, we don't know the TRUTH and how can we possibly handle it effectively, if we don't know the TRUTH. As a sales professional, I would recommend handling the person, not the objection by saying 'I understand you need to think about it, if I wasn't 100% certain about something I would also need to think about it; out of curiosity, what is causing you to hesitate?' By making the initial statement it shows empathy and by asking the open question, it allows the prospect to open up and tell you the TRUTH; only then are you in a position to deal with it.

You will sometimes hear a condition; this can be confused as an objection, however the difference is this is 100% out of your control. An example of this for my sales training company is, a prospect may state that they need a qualification when they have completed one of my sales training courses. We do not offer any qualifications; so I would need to understand why they feel they NEED a qualification, is this absolutely crucial in their decision process and once I understand the answers to both those questions, I can establish if its an objection or a condition. If its a condition, I simply move on and invest my time elsewhere.

The main reason you need to handle the person, not the objection, is you have to unlock the truth first. If a prospect or a customer says 'your product is too expensive' what are they actually saying? Do they mean they don't feel its worth that amount? Is it that they can't afford that amount? Does the amount fall out of their current budget? Are they comparing the price to a similar product from your competitors? Without understanding the real reason, I am unable to handle it. To uncover the truth, I would pose the question this way "when you say it's too expensive; what do you actually mean by that?" You should then get one of the four reasons I mentioned above and each needs to be handled different as follows:

Answer: I don't feel it's worth that amount

✓   From what we have discussed, where do you not see the value?

Answer: Can't afford that amount

✓ What budget did you allocate for this product? What part would you like us to remove from our service?

✓ What alternatives do you like the look of that falls within your budget?

Answer: The amount falls out of their current budget

✓ If you had the budget for it, would you go ahead? (good close) Great, well based on that when does your next budget start? We can take part payment now and the balance from your next budget.

Answer: Comparing the price to a similar product from your competitors

✓ Which product are you comparing this too?

✓ What is that product priced at?

✓ What are you actually getting within that price?

✓ Okay well for only £x (focus ONLY on the difference between your competitors price and your price) you are getting.... (highlight the features and benefits your product has over your competitors one.

Another technique in this scenario is to take price out of the equation by saying "if both products were priced the same which would you choose?" If they choose your competitors, then price was never the real objection. If they choose yours, ask them why? Then say for ONLY £x (the difference in price ONLY) isn't it worth spending that tiny but more?

Below I have written a list of objections that my clients have received and I have written the rebuttal below them:

Not interested

✓ Okay things have obviously changed since we last spoke, what has changed?

Too busy

✓ I understand that, so when is a convenient time to speak? Can I take your mobile number as well please

Happy with current supplier

✓ I appreciate that, who do you currently work with?

✓ How long have you been working with them?

✓ Who else did you look at in the market and why did you choose co X?

- ✓ What do they do for you and how's it working?

- ✓ How do you measure the results?

- ✓ What areas do you feel co X could improve?

- ✓ What 3 things would you make you consider looking elsewhere?

- ✓ When did your review the market to ensure you're getting the best product and service and paying the right price?

Too expensive or no budget

- ✓ Putting costs aside, on a scale of 1 – 10, 10 being exceptional levels of service where do you currently rate them?

- ✓ When you say too expensive, what are you comparing it too? (Sell the difference)

I need to speak to my business partner/ boss

1. I appreciate that, putting your partner aside, are you 100% comfortable with everything we have discussed?

2. Great, so I haven't missed anything you are looking at… (Summarise)

3. Organise a 2nd call to get feedback on conversation with partner to discuss moving forward.

Bigger rebate from competitor

✓ Putting the rebate to one side, how do you find working with them?

✓ What areas do you feel co X could improve?

✓ What 3 things would you make you consider even looking to change?

Bad experience with your company

✓ I am really sorry to hear that, what happened?

✓ What areas do you feel could have been improved?

✓ I understand how you **feel**, my client (name of co) **felt** exactly the same, however what they have now **found** with us is ... (give an example that puts their mind at rest and is relevant to their concern)

Send me information

✓ Our literature is very generic, I will send you information, however to ensure I make it relevant what specifically do you need to see?

✓ We both know you are not going to read it, it will be far more beneficial for us to meet so I can give you an idea of the savings we could offer you and how we can improve your service. I am available Tuesday or Thursday, which day is best for you?

Have a Preferred Supplier List

✓ Great, how do I get on that?

✓ Who is currently on it?

✓ Who gets involved in choosing the supplier from the PSL?

✓ What are your three key priorities when choosing a partner?

Have a National Agreement

✓ Who is that with?

✓ Aside from yourself, who else chose them?

✓ What products or services do you get with them?

✓ How do you find working with them?

✓ What products or services are you not getting from them that we could help you with?

Shopping around

✓ I think that's very sensible, can I ask what will you be basing your decision on? (Arrange the follow up call)

9: FAB SELLING

People only buy benefits, not features. When you talk about the value of your products or services, you are talking about the benefits, when you are talking about the costs, you are discussing the features.

People don't buy a drill, they buy a hole.

Now it's known that people buy with their emotions first and logic second, however people buy for different reasons. Therefore, before you share the features and benefits of your products and services, you need to understand what's important to your prospective customer. An effective way of finding this is out is asking "What are your top three priorities when choosing a X partner?" And then zip up and let the prospect really open up and share. You then have the information you need to tailor your feature and benefit pitch.

When discussing the relevant feature and benefits of your products or services on the perfect sales call, the focus must always be on "WIIFM" - What's in it for me?" Therefore if you understand what's in it for your prospect, you are able to tailor your pitch accordingly. You don't want to share anything that is not relevant to them and could turn them off your company.

The most effective way to turn a feature into a benefit is to add these two words at the end of the feature "which means" or "which enables". Let me illustrate this: Most companies like the fact we deliver bespoke sales training, because it gives your sales team the exact words to use for their everyday challenges, WHICH MEANS they achieve better results.

Now in the table below, list 10 features about your products or services and write the benefit next to it.

Once you understand what's important to your prospective customer, only then must you share the relevant features and benefits.

Feature	Benefit 'which means'
1	
2	
3	
4	
5	
6	
7	
8	
9	
10	

10: POSITIVE WORDS

When I had my first sales training about sixteen years ago, I was asked by the trainer 'how are you?' and I responded 'not bad'. He looked at me with disgust and said "well that's not great is it?" I didn't really understand what his problem was, however he made the point that people don't like talking to negative people and you must always come across in a positive manner; this can be achieved by your body language and the positive words you use.

In the table below I have written negative words on the left and the positive alternative on the right hand side to demonstrate how easy it is to use negative language. I would make a bet you currently use more of the words on the left hand side.

Negative words	Positive words
Sorry to keep you waiting	Thank you for waiting
I'm afraid/ unfortunately	At present/ Alternatively
But	And
I hope /I think	I'm sure/ I trust
Don't worry	Please be assured
No problem	Certainly/ My pleasure
Don't hesitate	Please feel free
Convenient to speak?	Thanks for taking my call
Feedback	Valued thoughts and opinions

Its imperative that you start to use positive words on every call and in your email correspondence. In the table below, please write down words or phrases that you want to use on a regular basis.

Positive words and phrases

11: Gaining Commitment and Closing

On the perfect sales call, you always require an objective of the call. We spoke earlier about the GAP of the call (Goal, Angle, Prepared) and dependent on what your goal is will depend on the close you use.

If your objective is to make an appointment, then prior to the call you need to select two to three dates when you are available to meet the prospect. Once you have qualified the prospect effectively you would say "I am available Tuesday and Thursday next week, which day us best for you?" I suggest you avoid the 'I'm in your area' line as most people are wise to that now and it also gives the impression that they are not that important to you, as you are in the area anyway.

Once the prospect has selected a date, provide them with two different times and I recommend choose quarter to or quarter past the hour, as it gives the impression you're busier i.e. what's better, 09:15 or 15:45?

People try and overcomplicate closing by using a variety of techniques, such as the assumptive alternative negative preventative close. I suggest KISS – Keep It Simple Stupid and ask for the business or the appointment, again dependent upon your objective.

My business partner and I recently analysed our business figures in minute detail to identify trends. One thing we noticed is my partner seemed to win the business in the first meeting more times than I did. I would normally win the business about a week after the first meeting, by sending out a proposal and arranging a follow up call to gain the prospects feedback and organising sales training. Guess what my business partner did in the first meeting that I didn't?

He asked for the business. KISS

At the end of the meeting my partner would say "it makes sense to me, does it all makes sense to you?" Once the prospect agreed it all made sense, my partner would say "great, so what dates would be convenient for you and your sales team?" And that's it; no clever formula or hypnosis involved.

Here's how I did it; at the end of the meeting I would say, "do you think I'm the right trainer for your sales team and for your business?", and when the prospect replied yes, I would wrongly say, "great, well I'll get a proposal over to you and then call you on X date to gain your valued thoughts and opinions and discuss moving forward". So I would walk out without a deal and it was all my fault, as I forgot to ask for the business. This was great feedback for me and funny enough I now win much more business in the first meeting.

In the table below, write down the words you like to use or techniques you are comfortable with to close the prospect.

| |
| |
| |
| |
| |
| |

12: CONCLUSION

You have every tool and technique you need now to make the perfect sales call, the rest is down to you.

Most people dread picking up the phone and find it a terrible experience, and I believe the main reason for this is they have not been given the techniques and words to use that have been proven to guarantee success that you now possess.

Sales is just a game; the better you get at the game, the more fun it becomes. The more you practice the game, using the right techniques that you have now learned, the better you become.

Not every call will go as planned, that's not real life, however take on board the feedback you receive so you can learn from every experience and use that on your next call.

Go out there and get your hit list prepared of who you want to work with and start making hundreds of perfect sales calls.

Lightning Source UK Ltd.
Milton Keynes UK
UKHW04f0738180918
329097UK00001B/470/P